OUT OF SOMETHING UGLY

MICHAELA BELMONT

writing as margot nothing

Out of Something Ugly

Copyright © 2020, 2017 by Michaela Belmont, margot nothing.

All rights reserved. This book or any portion thereof may not be reproduced or used in any manner whatsoever without written permission of the author except for the use of brief quotations in a book review.

Second edition 2020.

ISBN: 978-0-9995726-2-7 (Paperback)
ISBN: 978-0-9995726-3-4 (Ebook)

Library of Congress Control Number: 2017958990

Requests for permission or further information can be sent to info@michaelabelmont.com.

Cover image used under license from Shutterstock.com (artist Amanda Carden).

www.michaelabelmont.com.

Dedicated to Buddy the Cow Kitty.
I wish you were still here.

TABLE OF CONTENTS

INTRODUCTION ....
POETRY (52 TOTAL) ....

    Jester of My Nightmares (Feb 2007) 1

    As the Flowers Do (Jun 2007) 2

    HELLBOUND (Jul 2007) 4

    Gorge Crucial Thyme (2007) 5

    Mistake (Sep 2007) 7

    Revolting Lamentations (2007) 9

    He Died Last Week (Oct 2007) 11

    Gardwaffle (May 2008) 13

    All the Days (Jul 2008) 15

    Surviving Sacramento (Aug 2008) 17

    Write it Out and It's Yours Forever (2008) 18

    tears and blood (2011) 20

    Safe in the Dark (Apr 2016) 21

    Together, Part 1: Rain (Jul 2016) 23

    Reunited Brothers (Jul 2016) 24

    Etched (Jul 2016) 25

    Not Dead (Jul 2016) 26

    Together, Part 2: Night (Jul 2016) 27

everything and nothing (Jul 2016) 28

Something Sacred (Aug 2016) 29

Daylight (Aug 2016) 31

Reaching Inside (Aug 2016) 32

Tepid (Aug 2016) 33

Small Spark in a Black Bog (Aug 2016) 34

Perpetual Autumn (Sep 2016) 35

The Day You Cried (Oct 2016) 37

This Went On Too Long (Oct 2016) 38

Beautiful Dark (Oct 2016) 42

Something Beautiful (Nov 2016) 44

Hold On to It (Nov 2016) 46

The Tree Grows from the Root (Nov 2016) 47

My Baby Roscoe (Jan 2017) 50

Squirrels in the Road (Feb 2017) 52

BUDDY (Feb 2017) 54

The Temple Lies Empty (Mar 2017) 55

This empty grayscale place (Mar 2017) 56

Rip it Retch it Pull it OUT (Mar 2017) 57

The Sailor and the Serpent (Mar 2017) 58

The Old Dance (Jun 2017) 59

Heavy Melancholy (Jun 2017) 61

Blue Pieces and Blood Feeding: It Was So Long Ago (Jul 2017)
...... 62

Disfigured (Jul 2017) 63

Owl Doesn't Know How to Belong (Jul 2017) 64

Workshop (Aug 2017) 66

Raining Gray (Sep 2017) 68

Blasphemy (Sep 2017) 69

Water from Stone (Sep 2017) 71

Comfort (Sep 2017) 72

Giant (Oct 2017) 74

Freeze and Strangulation (Oct 2017) 75

Buddy's Grove (Oct 2017) 79

Once (Oct 2017) 81

THE END ....

INTRODUCTION

For the second edition of this book one of my main goals was to include an introduction. This is because when I first published *Out of Something Ugly* I was too apprehensive to put my work into context, or indeed say anything about myself at all. It came very naturally to me to hide. This is also partially why I originally published this book under the name margot nothing. I was afraid of my life, feelings, and thoughts being subject to public scrutiny, and also afraid of what my father might do if he found out I had written about him. I therefore found it comforting and safe to hide behind an identity of being nothing and no one. Something small.

This book emerges from deep personal experience. I was abused by my father in just about every way fathomable until I was fourteen. My earliest memories are from when I was a toddler, and it was already happening then. Whenever I tried to tell anyone I was either not believed or not understood. I have also been sexually abused by other perpetrators and have been in my fair share of unhealthy friendships in the years since. Marked harmful effects of the abuse and accompanying neglect included low feelings of self-worth, anxiety, depression, and struggling to have faith in anyone or anything. It can be hard to believe in anything when your own parent does that to you. It also makes it hard to trust. Self-blame has been another big one - as a young child you cannot wrap your head around the concept of a parent doing that because *they* are damaged. At that age you can only internalize it as *I must have done something wrong. He would not be doing this to me if I was lovable.* And that becomes the template that you use in every traumatic event that comes after.

Probably the most far-reaching unfortunate yet inevitable side effect was the formation of a victim identity. All I knew how to do was suffer, and so it played out over and over again. I attracted people into my life who disrespected and abused me, and I unfortunately did not know how to stand up for myself or that I was worth standing up for. After feeling beaten down to the point of near emptiness I would eventually walk away from long-term toxic friendships, but because I had not developed the confidence and self-love needed to set boundaries and assert myself I would end up in new ones. The same goes for short-term abusers – one after another after another. I was on that hamster wheel for a long time.

I thought that my suffering made me a good person. I also thought that if I labored and suffered long enough I would "earn" someone coming along to take care of me the way I tended to take care of others. It obviously did not work out that way. And perhaps subconsciously I knew that it would not – since I did not believe I deserved to be taken care of I was instead drawn to those who were more damaged and in more need of nurturing than I was. A never-ending illusion, an unending pursuit of the day when I would cease being the rescuer and instead be the rescued.

These poems are, for the most part, about surviving my father and the road to healing that I have been on for a very long time. A few are about other abusers that I have had, while others are ruminations over general discontent and are more societal in nature. A couple are fictional and detail their characters' relationships and processing of abuse.

Some are homages to beloved pets that have passed away. I wanted to memorialize them because of the impact they had on my life. I credit the animals I have known as being some of the biggest contributors to my resilience. I do not think I would be as capable of being warm and nurturing today without having had those bonds, and the lessons that came with them.

Several of the poems are about the first boy I was in love with, a boy who I am fairly certain loved me back but who treated me terribly. There are also a few about a particular group of friends that I had for a few years there in high school. I believe these friends cared about me as much as they were capable of at the time, but they unfortunately had no respect for me at all. We were all psychologically and spiritually wounded and had been abused. Some of us were still in abusive environments during the course of the friendship. It is no surprise, then, that we stuck together like glue. Like most dysfunctional families we all had our unhealthy roles, or identities within the group serving to help the group function. The role I embodied was that of the kind motherly nurturer who kept everyone together and who always put herself last.

When things were good, they were really good. But when things were bad, they were really bad. The strongest example of this is found in the months leading up to the end, as well as the months after. The group dynamic turned toxic and abusive, secretive and conforming, and I felt like I no longer recognized my friends. The hostility seemed random and impersonal at first. I did not wade into the fray myself - I instead retreated into wounded melancholy, to which the others responded by bullying and excluding me specifically. After a while I couldn't take it anymore, and when the dust settled they were on one side and I was on the other. I had chosen to walk away and so had become their common enemy. They hounded me for a long time after that.

I felt so wounded, and so betrayed, for so long. I had various complicated theories as to why they had turned cold towards me, over the years. But it has been over a decade, and the pain is now minimal. Now most days it is enough for me to simply shrug and say I do not know why I lost those friends. It is possible that they pushed me away because I was no longer one of them. I was beginning to go in a different direction at that time ... perhaps in a direction they themselves were not yet ready to go. I think I was beginning to take my first steps towards getting well.

One wonderful thing that I can say about my life, something that I am so grateful for, is that it has been almost entirely on an upward trajectory. To be frank, it did start off near the bottom. But that is still a very good thing. As painful as losing those friends was, my life and self-understanding evolved immensely after we parted ways. The severing was sudden and brutal, with a great deal of drama and blood. But when the scar came it was clear and raised, and I was stronger and more resilient for it.

With that boy that I was in love with the pain was different. For the first six months of our knowing each other he bullied me very badly. My self-esteem was low enough for me to blame myself for the way he treated me. After we fell in love he stopped bullying me, and could be kind when no one else could see. But he kept me a secret from everyone. I think perhaps he was afraid of what other people would think – worried that he would be considered a freak if he fraternized with a goth poet like me. He would not admit to his preppy friends that he loved me, or even that he knew me.

I do not think I need to delineate the pain this caused. Yet I hung on for six years, even after high school. When I finally let go, after years of tolerating the disrespect and loneliness, I felt as beaten and shapeless as if I had been dragged along the ground by horses. I was a flattened stump, devoid of defining features or hair. But I knew a lot more about love. I also knew a lot more about self-respect.

I used to think that suffering was an oversight on the part of God or whoever had created the world. I thought that it was something that should not be happening, that it would be addressed and rectified in due time. When that did not happen, when my and others' suffering kept occurring and the world just kept on spinning, feelings of despair and hopelessness were the result. If the world was not going to be made right, then I could not be happy. I thought I had no choice but to suffer unendingly and accept that there could never be any happiness in my life.

I understand now that suffering is part of life. Rather a large part of it, in fact. Happiness and suffering exist in tandem. So far from being an oversight needing correction, or a disease needing a cure, suffering is the material by which we change and grow and become more aware as human beings. Suffering can be the ultimate catalyst for growth, if we are willing to let our suffering teach us.

I had similar misconceptions about love. I thought love was a beautiful, shining thing, where those involved were always kind and respectful towards each other. Anything else, I thought, was an abomination and not real love at all. And so I spent a long time thinking that no one had ever loved me. I know better now. I also know that I am worth a higher quality love than what I have accepted in the past.

Love is not always light and pure. Sometimes it is brutal, and dark, and scrambling. Sometimes it is figuring things out by trial and error. Sometimes you treat the person you care about most in the world like absolute shit and you do not realize it for years. The point of love, like suffering, is growth and change. It is not meant to be pretty; it is meant to be transformative.

Those friends may have hurt me beyond imagining, but during the good times they also accepted me, supported me, and made me feel like I was not alone. For a couple of years there I knew what it felt like to belong. It was the first time in my life that I had felt that. At its best the group was a family, at its worst it was a cult ... and I shall never see something of its like again.

That boy may have broken my heart repeatedly and thrown the rags of my self-esteem into the trash. But he also loved me and saw things in me that no one else had before, which brought some light into a life that was very dark at the time. That opened my heart and my eyes, and I saw things I never thought existed. I became aware of a level of spiritual connection that I had not known was possible before. So both the good and the bad are true.

The aim of this book has always been to take ugliness and transform it, craft it, into something beautiful. To make something worthwhile come out of my pain and bad experiences. I want you, the reader, who has known suffering to know that you are not the only one who has felt like this, and that you are strong enough to survive it and become more than you ever thought you could be. I want you to have hope. I have come further in these past few years than I ever thought possible. I am no longer hiding in my family home, afraid of the world and convinced of my own worthlessness. I no longer feel like a defective alien, or like a stain on the planet's surface. I know my worth, and that I am sacred. I want you to know how incredible you are too.

    We get hurt in love so we can learn what we will and will not tolerate. We learn to love better. We are betrayed so we can see how strong we really are; we betray so that our own weaknesses can be exposed to us. We experience loss so we can understand what is truly important. We learn to be grateful for what we have. We cause hurt and are hurt so that we can heal. The greatest gift of all is self-awareness. Through the pain you find yourself.

    This book reflects the phase of my life in which I was grappling with the pain, utterly lost in the dark of feeling powerless and not knowing why these situations were happening. It chronicles my journey of finding an identity as someone of worth and value, as well as an understanding of how the trauma from my past was recreating my present over and over. This book ends right as I am getting ready to leave that old world behind.

    Things have changed now. The titanic shift in my journey began shortly after I published the first edition of this book in late 2017. The place that I am at now is lighter, less frightening, and makes more sense. There is still pain, of course, but I feel like I have a lot more control over my life. I am better at loving and letting others love me, and also aware of my ability to co-create my reality and experiences. My next book of poetry will show all of that. But this one still has its place. This pillar can stand forever, to commemorate that I journeyed through those dark forests, and survived.

Be well, and good luck,
Michaela Belmont
1/4/20

POETRY

Jester of My Nightmares

This insanity
fighting its way in
claws of iron, teeth of sin
oh god that scratchy papery skin
fighting its way in

This monstrosity
throwing its weight against the door
roaring obscenities
digging heels into the floor
can't keep this up anymore
throwing its weight against the door

(oh god i'm not strong enough)

The jester of my nightmares
the monster grins again
bloody roses, blackened dares
hatred rules again

The jester of my nightmares
hark, hark!
glinting and rustling in the dark
watch out for its bite, not its bark
it's coming it's coming through the dark

The jester of my nightmares
hark, hark!
glinting and rustling in the dark
watch out for his bite, not his bark
he's chasing he's chasing through the dark

"NO, DADDY, NO!"

As the Flowers Do

Blackened flowers, blooming round the widened orbs of terror
Cut red swollen lips
Surely damnation is as apparent around her
As the blue spots of color on her neck

The masses stare, this freakish collage of color
Momentary renown
But the interest soon fades around her
As the flowers do, fading into

brown
black
blue
purple
yellow
fading into
brown
black
blue
purple
yellow

These vivid smudges of color
Are rich in excuse
This damnation around her
In radiant hues

brown
black
blue
purple
yellow
fading into
brown
black
blue
purple

```
yellow
```

These faded flowers of color
Are rich in excuse
This damnation around her
In dying, darkening hues

HELLBOUND

Blades of grass that face the mower
Fallen leaves that sink even lower
Into the dark gutters
Hearing the dark mutters
Of misery

Uncaring fists that plunder the flower
All the small rodents of the world cower
From the laughing fiends
That don't understand their own dark deeds
They laugh

And then the monsters turn on each other
Stranger on stranger and lover on lover
The tears on faces terrified
The eyes widened in horrors realized
The garden is burnt

One by one the blades of grass face the mower
And one by one the leaves fall even lower
The princess left up in the tower
The torn hurt blemished flower
All the creatures in mid-cower
And always the poor stupid fiends
That don't understand their own fiery deeds

Gorge Crucial Thyme

the footsteps gain their distance
rustling spider shutters hide
me in my last place
me in my last dwelling place

a voice hoarse from screaming
though only in the mind
wants to break the silence
cannot break the silence
(oh god i'm scared)
please
help me

eat until the insides burst
breath held until the edge of death
no sleep, no sleep for me
shhhhhh

good piece
good piece
good piece of me be gone
gone gone gone somewhere
where you can have a better life

(i love you)

hollow halls
i cannot see you
silent walls
i cannot hear you
the darkness lights my way
(my heart!)
the sun, the sun
close the door!
i cannot bear it
anymore

vomiting shudders sickened mutters
look into my mirrors
i found me there
i tied him there
and he is never getting out

good piece
good piece
good piece of me be gone
gone gone gone somewhere
where you can have a better life

away from me

Mistake

So much emotion, rushing through
this body, an empty vessel of doom
and despair, but in this one moment
It matters not, for the emotion
rushing through
is rushing through
through

Rotting tar of anxiety
caked to my insides
Dripping, hissing acid of inadequacy
streaming out my nose, ears and eyes

Evil, evil extra fat
Unevenly scattered are zits and tumors
And if you were to pop one
Enormous flies and foot-long worms
Skittering, scattering spiders

Soft skin, soft?
No, it's just stretching
until it hangs from my sagging, withering frame
with the tumors gently moving

Squishing noises when I move
Rotting creature, squelchy voice
Surely this creature, from the swamp muck
was awoken from its cave at the end of the earth
Skin flakes off in chunks

This repulsive thing shuffles
Dripping, oozing, lumbering along
The monster that eats all your nightmares
and then dares to hunger for your dreams

Why am I alive

Why do I live
Maybe it's because
when I see you
I forget what I am

So much emotion, rushing through
this body, an empty vessel of doom
and despair, but in this one moment
It matters not, for the emotion
rushing through
is rushing through
through

Oh god, I wish I could have you
I wish I was good enough
I wish I could be beautiful for you
I ... love you.

Revolting Lamentations

A timidly asked question, from these moth-bitten lips:
"is my disease so apparent?"

A million lifetimes this beast has cried
Acidic confessions onto its stinking hide
"won't someone kill it?
stab it, slaughter it, gut it?"
But that would involve touching it!
Filthy thing, a grotesque fling
Of everything unwanted in one mad swing of creation
Why won't someone kill it?
Because it's sickeningly amusing

From the time it was spawned
Gamboling, crawling, falling along
It ached for sunlight, and sometimes found patches
Spotlights on the forest's dark floor
Black swamp muck seemed only too fitting
The hissing bubbles spitting
The thing found itself swallowed
In misery it wallowed
Hoping to escape the contempt

But centuries passed, as they must always do
The swamp finally gave birth anew
To the foulest thing that ever craved love
To feel the warmth from the sun above
But you're too. Damn. Ugly!

It cries piteously and warbles
It begs for acceptance, in spite of its appearance
But some things are too monstrous and can never be allowed

Oh, why must it linger, reeking so?
Why does it look with those cataract eyes, why can't it just go?
Why does it bleat in those pathetic tones

Why can't it just be happy alone?
Make it go away, the alien freak
God the worst thing is to hear it speak!

It shuffles away, unwanted again
Something so repulsive cannot have friends
Its returned to the swamp, only to see
That its place of refuge has dried up, there will no longer be
Any hiding within its disgusting depths

So what now for this thing, this unwanted thing,
Lurching and crying, attempting to sing
No one will kill it, that would be too kind
So off it wanders till the end of time

A viciously asked question, from these gurgling lips:
"why can't I die?"

He **Died** Last Week

I don't want to sleep tonight

Whiskers quivering
Rabbit in the brush
Ears tensed
Eyes widened
Always fear the...hush

Gray skies with fickle rain
Apathy calling above and below
Drawing hearts to cover up the stain
Seems so very long ago

Two-edged knives with double blades
Swinging through life with a thirst for blood
Finding bared teeth and scars in spades
Age-old footsteps dried in mud

Fear the sound of heartbeats
Pounding all around
Huge-fanged demons take their seats
Massacre without a sound

I don't want to sleep tonight

The lover of all that lives has died
Someone finally pulled the plug
And all around there's nowhere to hide
Find stinking peace in holes you've dug

The monsters snap their jaws and fly
The prey runs, breathless
And constantly the graying sky
The absolute terror, deathless

Scream into the uncaring sky
Beg for it not to take you

**Pray to the dead mister you get to die
And to your dead Father, too**

(Dead, dead, dead)
He died last week

Whiskers quivering
Rabbit in the brush
Ears tensed
Eyes widened
Always fear the...hush

Oh, please don't make me sleep tonight

Gardwaffle

Before I begin to speak
Pitiful heart aching, misshapen body weak
I'm going to say that this is for you
The flowers I raised around me
Only to be bloodied by the thorns

I led a life of measured dread
Hiding within dark caverns
But I got a glimpse of something beautiful
And ventured outside to look

Such lovely blossoms, albeit ragged
Wounded by the elements or by design
Either way I took you in
To ease all our suffering

Such beauty in a life that saw it not
Is it no wonder I clung so dearly
Yet it would appear that flowers' hearts can be just as ugly
As any other

Now that I've begun to speak
This mocked gardener, all alone freak
I'm saying now that this is for you
Who left me alone in my hell

Ignored by the things I cherished
Why, why won't you look at me?
Screaming for attention, for love
From ice-cold petals and stems with sudden thorns

They stabbed me and were returned
To the land from which they came
Sometimes I peer out of my cave
Only to see them exactly the same

Alone a thousand years I tread

Without once a single friend
Such a foolish, ugly creature, I see
To think beautiful things could have ever loved me

Now I've finished speaking
I hope I'm remembered in your minds
Not because I'm all cut up
Or because I'm standing upon this rock
No, I want you to remember me only because
I'm the loneliest gardener there ever was

All the Days

When the world began spinning by, again
I saw you
Every day there ever was, again
I miss you now, again

Take this day away from me
Take every day I waste
I waste it for you anyway

These eyes that you longed to see
Lose tears you never thought were there
Or maybe you just didn't care
I wish I could take back every day you tainted

When the world got fuzzy, again
And I lost my way
What I found were the days
I'll never forget, again

I can forget everything except my love for you
It's spun through every day
I've never asked for much, but please
Just take these wasted days away

Sometimes the questions return
They buzz around my head
Sometimes fake smiles of you
Say the things you never said

But this doesn't matter and I need to stop
I can't let you torment me like this
I tell myself you're dead to me
But I don't believe it

When the world got familiar, again
And I felt myself feel okay

I saw you, again
I saw every single day

Surviving Sacramento

Part two to forgetting:
I'm remembering everything.
Little things I'd long ago grown weary of
Came back to remind me they were here all along

Reborn from the ashes
Just in time to be informed that new beginnings hurt
And no I don't need a map
This town beats in my heart

It pounds in my skull
I stumble around
Lost in this hell that loves me
Amazingly enough the feeling is bittersweet

I heard the world is ending in 2012
Wouldn't argue with before
This whole life has been an echo
Of something I always wished for

Watching my world change
Watching my people change
Years pass by in tears
I guess even bad things can't last forever
Amazingly enough the feeling is bittersweet

Write It Out and It's Yours Forever

I woke up and it's winter again
And not a new winter
The same one as before
And this rain cloud over my head
Is the exact same fucking one

Rain: a reminder of what summer forgot
Winter calls back the faces of yesterday
Finding only recycled thoughts
Spring was just a dream

People may be gone but their images remain
An autumn delusion, a holiday hallucination
Can't sleep for their voices but I found a solution
For this nostalgic condition

Look out the window and winter replays the scene
Same moments again in this waking dream
I miss those awful days, it's true
The strange thing is I don't miss you

The freezing air
Freshly straightened - and now wet - hair
Wandering the paths of our prison
To avoid going to our eventual destination
Not beautiful today, just a face
Can't sleep for her bitching so I'll just stare into space
Don't push me around
I'm already falling down
Help me out the door
Into the frozen freedom of before

Birthday's selflessness meets
Your Christmas selfishness
Which started the trend
Of mistreating friends

And two winters of cowardice from *you*
Was, unfortunately, nothing new
But apparently there was still something to lose

People may be gone but their images remain
An autumn delusion, a holiday hallucination
Can't sleep for their voices but I found a solution
For this nostalgic condition

Autumn delusion (holiday hallucination)
Can't sleep for their voices (but I found a solution)
Missing those awful days (but not you)
For this nostalgic condition
I found a solution

tears and blood

always cried a lot. i remember that much. where do tears go, exactly? do they just evaporate where they fell, into denim, into skin? or do they sink in, forever staining, albeit invisibly, changing the surface that's absorbed them, infinitely? i wonder a person made of tears. one of my worst fears, a person who puddles at my feet. but what of someone who never cried? a person who's said they've never cried is someone who is made of lies. but would that make them a person of tears, since they've never cried them out? or have they simply dried out, a soulless hunk of flesh, of moistureless meat? room temperature, or filled with heat? i wonder what i am. i don't really remember who i am from one moment to the next. oh well. i've read many a text, but no answers yet. oh well, oh well. i've so many hours left, to ponder this out. so many knives, to bleed it all out. is blood like tears, or something else entirely? does blood free the misery from inside me? am i made of blood? i never saw blood. only tears. mayhap i'd prefer to cry, or mayhap i'd prefer to die. does blood forever change where it lands? oh my bloody hands, so many surfaces they've stained. so many inches of skin maimed in this fruitless hunt for knowledge. if you have a wound, can you cry them back shut?

Safe in the Dark

Have you ever heard the wailing in the dark

A dark, glorious cacophony
while you're wrapped in your cocoon

I'm safe here, they can't find me <whispered>

Am I the predator or the prey?
I think both, because even with that warm
blood running from my jaws I'm hunched,
looking over my shoulder.

I'm so afraid of seeing my blood
dripping from something's smirking mouth

It's so cold here
Though the temperature's all right
It's midnight
It's always night
I'm hidden
Safe in my cocoon
My bedroom
It doesn't feel like you

In this dark I can be anything at all
(I can be anything in the dark.)
I can be a little girl, cradled in an embrace
I can be a monster, TEARING THEM APART

It's so cold here
Though the temperature's all right
It's midnight
It's always night
I'm hidden
Safe in my cocoon
My bedroom

It doesn't smell like you

I hear the broken and inverted -
The corruptions and the twisted.
It protects its own, and their delusions.
And I hear that howling silence.

<we're all here>
<there's so many of us>
<it's so peaceful>
<i'm safe>

Together, Part 1: Rain

Reduce me to nothing
reduce it all to rage and pain
strip away the noise
of the everyday

Strip away the day
strip away what protects me
and bare me
to the moonlight
and your monstrous machinations
and what you find ... destroy
the soft things, the weak things, the warm things – destroy
the pink things, the pale things, the special things – destroy
wash away the mundanity with sweat and tears
that daylight drudgery, the haze of color and dust
consumed by the dark sudden rush
of this moment

Nothing but animals
wash the humanity away

This rain of sin and horror
washes away my life

Reunited Brothers

You see those ice blue eyes looking at you, and you
know they're as cold as his heart. But
he's looking at you and he's happy to see you and
you can't help but start
moving towards him, arms reaching out.
He's moving towards you too, and while his mouth
is moving you can't make out the sounds
that are coming out of his throat.
But that's alright because you know they're warm. You haven't
seen him in so long and
surrounded by this throng of people you have never met
This is as beautiful a reunion as you could ever get.

The people in this crowd are scared, they're frightened.
There's been bombs and famine. Like always he's calm as a port
in a storm and like always he's got a plan. "We're gonna
head to Wichita," he says, clapping you on the back. The smile
he's giving you and the hug you've just shared
has made you an amnesiac. He laughs at the tears you're
trying to blink back ...
but he doesn't laugh too hard.

You ask him why he's here, wasn't he nearer to the opposite
foamy coast? "I came for you, you silly goose" – you
don't care if it's true. Even if not you feel it in
your heart, this warm bond, attachment, and
after this long, lonely absence
you can almost convince yourself
that he feels it too.

Etched

They say time heals all wounds but that isn't really true
Some scar over into these purple mounds,
jagged lines running over you
And you remember the red horses
stampeding down when they were new.

These wounds change your surface.
They change the shape of you.

*You all are etched
into my flesh
And yet I feel I've had no effect
on yours*

Even with the long dried-up riverbank of tears,
and even while memory's lines and colors smear,
I still find that all these years
haven't made this pain disappear.

Not Dead

A flower, alone, sat dead for so long; withered, grey, wilted.
Its defeated head nearly touching the ground.
So many years, silence; surrounded by decay; just ghosts, and more ghosts, echoing grey. But suddenly, inexplicably, a slight rising up, gentle; and breaking from the greyscale is one softly pink petal.

Together, Part 2: Night

></br>
> We're laying naked in bed together
> I'm looking over at him
> I want to scoot closer but I'm afraid to
> Closed eyes
> but that clenched, hateful face

I feel her moving closer to me ...
she thinks I'm asleep.
She's resting her head on my chest now,
I breathe in deep
the smell of her hair, I'm always finding long strands
of it everywhere
She is mine, forever.
She's never leaving me.

> The moon's reflection reclaims
> the jewel on his dagger.
> The one that almost took my life.
> I see it on the nightstand
> But he slides his hand to the small of my back
> and everything feels safe.

everything
and nothing.

I am the disgusting fat girl, weird and disliked
I am the beautiful, crying princess, hurt and desirable
I am the cruel cretin that spits in their faces
The monster who slinks into their most private places
I am everything
And I am nothing

The hero, rushing in to save them all
I'm the coward, frozen and afraid
The charming manipulator, controlling it all with
a flick of the wrist
I'm the idle, useless daydreamer
imagining all of this

I get lost everywhere except in my own head
That's because I can't find it
I don't know
where it went
I know how to be so many people
but which one is me?
Am I in here somewhere or
did I throw myself out?

Something Sacred

Warm, only slightly feathered over wrinkled skin
The baby pigeon stumbles forward
Loudly cheeping, little vestiges of wings flapping
A sweet, expectant smile on its dorky yellow face.

No longer alone,
Softly pecking at that which approaches
Mouth ready to open
Eagerly trusting
and prepared to be taken care of.

But the hand comes down and tweaks a wing instead.
OW! A cheep of pain – but it must have been an accident.
After a moment of confusion, the pigeon returns to its begging.

But the hand comes again and snaps the wing this time.
The baby screams, stumbling away, terror
overtaking its hunger.
It doesn't understand what's happening.

The baby's hiding next to a garbage can now
Eyes glassy and afraid, desperate for protection.
To the giant, looking down, surely this pitiful image must
foster some kind of nurturing feeling.
The baby weakly moves its good wing, a pantomime of
the food-begging behavior from earlier.
It cheeps, softly.
As the hand comes again, the baby feels a slight resurgence
of hope, of trust
begin to blossom into forgiveness.

But the hand comes down and snaps the other wing.
Horror overtaking this baby, screaming, panic.
The giant watches it try to waddle away, watches its suffering.
Then it pins it under its shoe

and slowly
crushes it.

Blood's coming out of the baby's eyes, and mouth.
Life and, more importantly, something sweet and innocent,
destroyed.
Just a smushed collection of bones and guts, now.
And the giant merely observes this
and then gets back in its car
and drives away.

Daylight

That place where things are dark and hopeless
where you have no hope for love
where people are raped and where they commit rape
you live there
you do

That dark place
where having that done to you was unavoidable
where it was just ... part of life
where the humiliation and pain was just a staple
of an existence built on survival

you don't have to live there
you can escape
you can come out
to the sunlight
and wash that darkness
off of you

wash that sickness off
in the daylight

You don't have to stay in the dark
Please, don't stay in the dark

Reaching Inside

I reach into my chest,
grab this beating, bleeding hunk
of mess and pain, and rip it out
and press it between these pages

I do it because I want this
blood and gore on *your* hands
I want this to jump into your chest and
contort *your* beating, bleeding core
I want you to feel something

Please understand what I'm screaming out
Please see what I'm digging out
Look at me, ripping this out of this cavity
Please see me
and understand what I'm about.

This pain ... this loneliness ...
THIS SCREAMING!
MY EYES! MY EYES!
I'M GOUGING OUT MY INSIDES
DO YOU SEE IT?!

Tepid

I can't be what you want.
I can't be what you need.
I'm just a shadow, a shape filled with shallow
sand, visible under the tepid few inches of river water, a
hollow empty sack.
All I do is fail and disappoint every person I meet.
I can't be what you need.

I don't have anything
to offer anybody.

Small Spark in a Black Bog

There was a spark of something human,
somewhere in the midst of miles in that quagmire.
But in the black and wet and stench and rotting
there was nothing dry for that spark to catch.

Lost inside the miles of muck in that quagmire
I tried to find that spark ... I tried to make it catch.
Little girl, armed only with naivety, foolish trust
and toddling legs.

Trapped in that quagmire, by unseen black walls
Covered with disgustingness and a sock stuffed in my mouth.
Eyes wide with tears and from mouth a wailing cry
I failed, I failed
And there's no one to turn to.

Nobody's responding to my echoing cries.
No matter where I look there's ... nobody ... in sight.
Everything's ... silent.

Perpetual Autumn

Cover me with autumn leaves
Soft blue sky overshadowed by setting sun
pushing wispy bits of cloud away

So quiet, muted.
Stay like this until I die.
This is the same autumn day as so long ago.
I'm a child, still.

Daddy, you betrayed me.
But I accept the past.
I think in your sick way you loved me
But even if you didn't
I loved you
And that's all that matters.

I own this pain.
It belongs to me.
The suffering you brought
to me, I own and control it.
The past, it belongs to me.
I guess it belongs to you too.

Cover me with these autumn leaves
I'll fade away, along with these muted colors
A lifetime of quiet, and then I'll die
And the world will never know the difference.

Cover me, silently, autumn leaves, bury me
And I'll sleep for a century.
And when I wake it will still be this understated, autumn day
Fading into evening.

I loved you, Daddy.
I loved you very much.
Even now, sometimes,
You're all that matters to me.

And the pain you wrought, it belongs to me.
I own it all.

I don't want anyone to ever see me.
I don't want anyone to see my face.
I want to stay in my peaceful, quiet place
And then fade away when I die.
I want to sleep this long sleep
Until I wake.

An unimportant figure, in the big scheme of things,
writes this to you from beyond the grave.
It says, "I wasn't very important, in the big scheme of things.
You don't know my name, or face.
You've never heard of me, I'm just another soul lost to history
But I loved someone very much,
And that's all that matters."

The Day You Cried

I remember the day I saw you cry.
I was only three then, I think.
You were hunched over the steering wheel, sobbing noisily.
You were saying, "I'm sorry, I'm sorry."
And you said my name.

My own cries went quiet.
I was shocked, alarmed.
There is nothing so scary, so compassion-inducing
as seeing God fall apart.

I reached for you.
I couldn't connect.
My stubby little toddler arms
weren't good for much.
But I reached out, I tried
because I wanted to make your pain subside.
And I think that was the only time
you ever looked like a human being.
Like a hurting soul
with something beautiful inside.

This Went On Too Long

You wouldn't believe how many lines I've written
trying to say what I want to say to you.

Choppy lines of bitterness, resentment and hate
blasting my rage at being misused and mistreated.
Long flowing poetry, with reliable rhyming
in which I attempt to be so forgiving and gracious about it all.
And of course, of course, spattered throughout
are the shorter works of weepy self-pity.
In them I'm but a hurt child again,
a demanding, needy victim, lonely.

Some of them are good.
Most of them are drivel.
But I've realized that, at least when it comes to you
the more I write, the less I say.

Maybe that's because I never did understand you.
You always were a Rubik's Cube encircled by a combination lock.
So, like most fools who don't understand something
I've talked on and on about it, trying to convince myself
I get it.

But I don't.
I loved you – this I know.
And I think you loved me too.
But I never understood you – why you bullied me,
why you pretended not to know who I was,
why you denied me.
I don't know why you refused love.

So I'm trying to keep it short.
For once, in my life, trying to keep my writings about you
short.
Loving you was excruciating, I'm sure you know that.
You didn't make it easy to love you, but I was nothing
... if not up for a challenge.

The things you said to me, I cut myself over them.
And when I got kicked out of our school, for about six months
that was because I was ditching so much
because I was afraid of you.

You abused me. You treated me awfully.
And while it seemed like you tried to be better after that,
even your Improved You was a dick.
It was almost better to have you degrade me
than to pretend I didn't exist.

Those couple times that I've seen you,
in the past few years
you looked at me like ... nothing had changed.
You looked like you still had the butterflies,
and I think your eyes still lit up.
As if we were still in high school.

But years had already passed since
I watched you parade all those girlfriends around
that you claimed not to love
Years had already passed since I wept alone,
needing you.
Those years were long over
and the love in me had died.

I can't believe it.
I'm crying again.
All these years later and thinking about you
still has the power to make me cry.
I wonder, do you know how worthless you made me feel?
Do you know the power you held in your hands?

A single word from you could silence me, shame me,
pulverize me.
You had complete control over
whether I had a good day or a bad day.

And yet all I concerned myself with was *your* pain, *your* day.
You owned my fucking heart.
Do you know that?

I don't have a clue. I don't know what you feel or don't feel.
I don't know how often you think about me,
or if you do at all.
I don't know why you refused me.
Did you not think I was good enough for you?
Were you afraid what people would think?
Did you not want to love anyone,
or think that you weren't worth loving?
Was there some deep, complicated reason for all of this ...
or was it just some stupid game of clique?

I'm afraid to know.
I'm afraid to never know.
I'm afraid to go through life attaching so much meaning to
something that I don't understand.
But I'm also afraid to know the truth
because what if it's just ... shallow?

The rage in me,
that burns towards you.
I'm
afraid
of that
too.
Afraid of how weighed down and grudgeful
it makes me, how hopeless and ugly it feels.
Although sometimes, it feeds me.
I look back on how you treated me
(which just so happened to be
exactly what I thought I deserved at the time)
and I think, never again.

And that is a definite understanding

that I've taken from all this pain.
I'm not going to chase after and wait loyally for
someone who won't even admit to knowing me in public.
I'm not going to pour endless quantities of love
into someone who gives me nothing in return.
Because I have discovered, at the end of this long, tired road
that I have worth.
I am a human being.

I'm so tired, T----.
So tired, and disillusioned, with all of this.
The love I felt for you was so beautiful, I wanted it to persist
until the end of this life, and into the next.
But it's gone.

I didn't want to believe
that something as transcendental as love could die.
But it did, years ago.
And it was such a mercy.

Beautiful Dark

I hear it calling me.
That beautiful melody, evoking such
a nostalgia in me.
Under the earth
deep under the waves
reaching outward from the pitch-black caves
calling me.

Down, diving, deep.
Under the waves
into the silence.
Descending the stairs,
ever further down.
That music, gently
--[insidiously]—
pulling me closer.

I know this sensuous, safe, comforting darkness
wants to consume me.
to corrupt me.
to destroy me.
It bears me no respect, no autonomy.
It wants me to feed it, and be fed
though I only get enough
to whet my appetite.

I can become all-powerful
but only by becoming a slave.
I can have all the ecstasy in the world
but without the soul to feel it.
I can be offered all the most grandiose of promises
only to reach out, shaking with the exertion, and grasp
ashes.

So
Beautiful.

Down, diving, deep.
Further.
Deeper
down. Don't look back.
Close your eyes and
let yourself become lost.
So
familiar.
It feels like
home.

Something Beautiful

He wasn't a god.
He was an antisocial pervert who always smelled bad.
He only felt powerful
when he was holding someone smaller down.
Or behind a computer screen
or video camera.
That was what mattered most in his life.

I wanted him to be a god. More than anything.
He was my ... dad, after all.
But he was just a -
I hesitate to say man.
An abused, sadistic smirk, light glinting off of Dahmer glasses.
Sweating in the shadows.
But he was also loneliness
and tears in beat-up Beatle cars.

"Autumn leaves" ... blah blah blah.
I just wanted to make something beautiful out of something
ugly.
That, if anything,
is what defines me.
The truth is that I will do just about anything
to make ugly reality beautiful.
I will make it so dramatic and tortured,
so twisting and complicated.
And maybe I'm not even wrong.
But sometimes it can be more simple than that.

I want to redeem unforgiveable things and
save sad and broken things.
I want to breathe life into dead things.
I want to create
     light
and pour it into the emptiness around me.

Maybe I desire this because I'm a beautiful soul.

(That would be lovely, right?)
But maybe it's more selfish than that.
Maybe I want to transform ugly things
because I don't know how to heal *myself.*

Even after all this time
I carry this heavy hatred
           and contempt
           and disgust
for myself.
And while on good days I try to breathe that life, that healing light
into me, most of the time

                            it fizzles out into nothing.

Hold On to It

I have to hang on to me
I have to keep it safe
I can't let anyone
destroy me
I have to keep it safe.

If he, if they, take it from me,
I'll lose all sense of self.
There'll be nothing left in here
but screaming winds across a black emptiness.
There'll be nothing.

I won't let him take this from me.
Hold on to it, keep it safe.
DON'T LET HIM DESTROY IT

The Tree Grows from the Root

Ugly things don't turn into beautiful things.
They can improve, sure.
But even with the butterfly's better body
those disgusting bulging eyes.
The tree grows from the root.

With my father, and with the boy I loved
I was hanging on to something hideous, in the hope that
it would transform
before my very eyes.
But with my father, hanging on didn't change the past
and with that boy, hanging on improved things
but it was still cruel and painful.

Contrast that with Buddy, the cat.
It was beautiful from the start.
I tried my best to take care of him
and he became the closest friend I ever had.
We had our rough patches, of course.
Like when I stepped on him on accident, hurt him, and he
took off and hissed at me.
Or when I would try to trim his nails, that scared him,
and he would bite and snarl and scratch at me.
But those ugly times were few and far between, and
Buddy was much kinder and more respectful to me
than either of those before-mentioned that I spent years, blood
and tears on.

If the basis is ugly, the rest will surely follow.
Love based on abuse and self-hatred cannot, by any definition,
evolve into that heaven you were craving,
where your worth is finally validated after all.
You won't find that in ugly places.

I want you to know that.
I want everyone to know that.
Someone mistreating you is not an objective

reflection of your worth.
It doesn't mean you're worthless.
It means that you're interacting with someone who needs to feed
on others' blood.
It means they need your submission and pain
to feel whole.
They're empty.
And it's up to you to decide
if you're going to allow yourself to be
what they feed on
to try to fill themselves up.

And yes – they're hurting.
That's why they do it.
But no, it doesn't matter.
They have no right
to torture you like that.
You're a human being.

Love growing from abuse.
That's all I know how to envision.
First, because I don't know intimacy any other way
and secondly because I would so love to turn
the hideous, nightmarish beginning of my life
into something beautiful.
But that's never going to happen.
I was molested, tortured, and hurt.
It was recorded.
Nothing is going to change that.
Nothing is going to make that tragically forgivable,
or compassionately understandable.
And no imagined down-on-his-knees apology
or revealed suffering of his own childhood
could ever fix this wrong for me.
There is no amount of sympathy I can throw on this wound
to clean it out.

Someone could theoretically abuse me

and either love,
or learn to love,
me.
But that wouldn't make the relationship beautiful.
It would still be a rotting, contorted trunk
with sickly black branches lashing out to the sky.
Still a misshapen, skittering insect
with clacking mandibles and bulging, glittering eyes.

Slow, painful epiphany, characterized by letting go of control:
What my father did to me
was not my fault.
What that boy put me through
was not my fault.
At all.

Buddy.
I'm so sorry you're gone.
I wanted more time.
And I see now that I've been hung up on the
wrong people for the longest time.
You are the only man I have ever loved
who has made me feel loved in return.

My Baby Roscoe

Let it be known that the day Roscoe died
The entire sky cried.

Six years, essentially your entire life
are what I got to spend with you.
And six years is a full life, for a guinea pig.
But even so, it's hurting really bad.
I wasn't ready
to say goodbye.
I'm sorry you were having a hard time breathing.
I'm sorry it hurt when they gave you that shot.
I'm sorry it was raining so hard outside, I know
the bad weather scared you.
I'm so sorry for every time I wasn't as much
as I should have been.
I hope I did right by you, Roscoe.
I hope I gave you a good life.

Let it be known that, as Roscoe slept
The entire world
wept.

If Buddy was my boyfriend then Roscoe was my baby.
You were my little baby.

You were always my baby.
So small, in my hands.
I rolled a marble in my hands;
I buried you with a dragonfly
and asked it to follow and help you
wherever your journey took you.

And I see now, in my mind's eye
Roscoe running across a never-ending field,
bright green except for the dandelions.
No shortness of breath to hold him back, now.
And as he races on, ecstatic, stops to eat or see something,

or sniff at the air,
I see he isn't alone.

Please take care of him, spirit.

Squirrels in the Road

Every day I see squirrels' bodies in the road.
People drive apathetically by, hordes after hordes of us.
I wonder, do those squirrels have families
nearby, mourning in the trees?
Why does the world keep on turning when
there is so much death?
Why are we all so separate?
Why do we not share pain?

I wonder despondently how sacred life can possibly be
when a little squirrel's body
gets driven over, countless times a day,
until it's a barely recognizable gray bump on the road.
And then, a little ways down the street,
there's another.
And another.

I've seen raccoons in the end stages of distemper.
One of the most horrible things I ever saw.
And the ones that I saw
had at least been brought in
so they could be euthanized.
But what about the others?
How can life have any kind of meaning
when a raccoon dies alone, in agony,
out in the wilderness?
Maggots eating it alive, from the inside
as though it had already died?
With no one around to care
or make the pain stop?

How can people observe suffering and not feel it themselves?
We do it every day.
Aren't we all part of some connected, greater ...
aren't we?
Then why is there such a disconnect?
Is this all life is, just selfish self-experience in an empty void?

I laugh at the TV in my house while my next-door neighbor,
weeping, ends his life in his?
Why are we all so separate?
Why do we not share pain?

Is this how things are supposed to be?

God is dead.
I saw the empty throne room.
I saw the sheets pulled over the hospital bed
with one weary, weathered hand hanging
down.

Yet we drive over the dead bodies of squirrels
every day and say hey, I'm alright.

BUDDY

I love you, Buddy.
It's been months, and I still cry over you.
You were the man of my life.
Not only did you let me love you ...
you made me feel loved in return.
I don't know if this ache is ever going to subside.
I wish, wish so hard, that we could have some more time.
I would sacrifice ten people in some eldritch ritual
to give you more time.
... or more, if it was called for.

I'm sorry your last day wasn't better.
I'm sorry that that you were in so much pain, and that
I didn't know how to help you.
I'm so sorry you were scared.
I'm sorry that I fell apart
when you needed me the most.
I love you, Buddy. I love you so
much.

The Temple Lies Empty

A love unrequited met with an anger uninvited
that set the tone for every note that followed.

Thick fingers wrapped around the greasy heart
Beating with desperation, waiting to start
to feel clean again, but this hand
squeezing and squeezing over and over again.

Colored adoration, sliding off of a cold objectification.
Unable to make it stick.
This idol is sick.
Any attempts to leave it gifts
break apart into dust.

It has been so long since the teeth bared wrong
and the silence has lost its echo.
But this heart won't start and the pain won't depart
because the hand belongs to the heart.

This empty grayscale place

An empty space
where once were litterings of clocks, wind-up toys
and bombs
lies still
and quiet.

This one stopped ticking – take it out.
This one stopped ticking – take it out.
And with each one picked up by the hand
and carried away, never to be seen again
a rumination ensues, soft and storming.

This place once had no empty space
for all the mechanisms buzzing within it.
But now this room is only a tomb
and even its ghosts are absent.

Rip it Retch it Pull it OUT

Listen to me. Prisoner, convict of your own hate.
So eternally angry and violent.
I know what you need.

I want you to reach inside and grab that brown-red
gnarled mass, pull that bloody
nest up out of your throat and
plop it down on the table.

Tell me why you hurt them. Tell me
what they did to you.

Tell me who you hate. Give me a name, a face.
Or a haircut, or a feeling. Whatever attachments you have,
give them to me.
Tell me why. Tell me what they did.
Make it visceral. Make it bloody. Throw out
the shroud of mundane, of matter-of-fact.
Make it ugly.

Scream it out.
This is yours.
It's so old, cords from it entwining in with your throat, and chest.
Break them.
This sick choking and retching will be worth it
for the empty, clean space freed inside.
I can help you – rip it out for me. Pull this
bloody ball out of your throat, gagging.
Throw it on the table.

Pull out your bloody mass.
Show it to me.
This catharsis
is unbelievable.
Rip it out.

The Sailor and the Serpent

Cast out to that golden serpent,
wide carnival smile and lost outside eyes
This pitiful message in a small, insignificant
bottle.
It'll never see it, it'll never see it.

Sad, lonely seaman, drunk and wobbling off
the shore
Reaching out, being surrounded
by those cold, uncaring coils
So desperate for touch he'll take anything,
even predation.

Do you remember me, fiend?
Gigantic serpent, twisting and grinning
in the waves.
Do you see me on the shore?
I've been out on a boat, before
when I was left by my friends to your sly
machinations.

I'm hurting, I'm hurting.
I'm in pain.
Is what the note reads.

I know a monster is a monster.
To expect better or different is foolish
and rooted firmly in wanting to change the past.
But, part of me still screams, monster
Can you give me some validation?

The Old Dance

Hey! We're going back to the old place!
Out of time and out of space!
Hey! We're doing the old dance!
Join us!

She's dancing in the circle, surrounded by the swaying shadows
She carries her knife in her teeth
Blood flies onto the ground and through the air
from the streaked wounds on her arms and legs
and face
as she spins

Join us!
In the circle, around the circle!

Blood!
Blood!
Blood!
Paint!
Paint the stone!

You might have forgotten it
but in the old places, these ageless faces
smile closed-eyed of harmonies never truly forgotten
This dance hasn't stopped
and it never will!

She's more blood than face
and her feet slide easily in the puddle of blood beneath her
that she splashes up.
Her hair's filthy, and her eyes are shining
and she's smiling

It's never stopped!
Come!
You can be part of this!

Hey! We're going back to the old place!
Hey! We're doing that old dance
of frenzy and blood and spins and turns
at the core of everything that's right and well
with the universe

Be born with us!
Be lost with us!
Come back to so long ago, in this forgotten pocket out of time.

There's no reason to leave.
You don't want to.
Don't worry – the dance will never stop.
And the world you came from will slowly spin away, dying and quiet
so muted and mundane and far away
without you.

Mauled and frenzy and unrecognizable!
Free and lost and undeniable!
She's more wound than flesh and they're more darkness than people
but
Hey!
Demons like to party too and you don't need all your body to dance.

Hey!
Hey!
Join us!
We're at the old places!
We're doing the ancient undying dances!

Heavy Melancholy

I am burdened with a heavy melancholy.
Always have been; today I asked myself
why.
The simple, easy answer DADDY comes
screaming shrill to the forefront;
But that is not the case.

This life has been an empty echo of something I
always wished for.
Nothing, no one, ever good enough.
You have people leeringly, proudly, tell stories
of the lies they told to coerce people into bed with them.
You turn on the news and there's a Brazilian orphanage
with girls burning alive, whose only crime was raging against adults
that didn't care about them. Police officers
kept them locked in the room
as they died.
So ugly. The deaths, the rapes. The lies.
Everyone and everything is a pitiful, shattered
caricature of what it should be.

Nothing is how it should be.
That's why I'm so melancholy.

My first time getting drunk shouldn't have
been that way. My friendships shouldn't have
been that way. My parents, relatives.
And me, too. I'm a disappointment, a hollow,
weak, tissue-thin mockery
of everything I should be.

Blue Pieces and Blood Feeding:
It Was So Long Ago

He took a chisel to my child chest
and, with the shattered blue exposed
he took out pieces of my soul.
He stole pieces of my soul.

He walked me, hand in hand
to an old shrine in the forest he knew, and
laid me up upon it.
Pained grimace upon his face as he
ripped my blood up out of me
and onto the encrusted stone.
I thought I screamed, but maybe I just
became
silent.

These things meant something, once.
And they still do, in their dedicated halls of memory.
They are framed, up on the walls, and playing, behind closed doors
but while once they were my life, my death,
my tears, and my abandon
they are now just ancient relics
in hallways that are gathering dust
and the pain, the power, is hallowed but a remnant
of what it used to be.

I have, in my hands, this red blood-crusted box
that I have carried for so long.
But while once it held agony, and love, and terror
I am starting to suspect that it does no longer.
I think I'm just carrying this box around
because it used to have something in it.

Disfigured

There are some fissures that are permanent.
The skin just has to grow back around them.
And make do.

There is a darkness inside, a flatness.
A cold black chasm, with screaming, sobbing winds.
A disfigured mountainside tore these fissures into me.
Sometimes I fall into that
bottomless pit inside.
I fall through the cracks of myself.

Upon the rending of the abyss, the crust ripped apart
and the pieces
hid
inside.

Owl Doesn't Know How to Belong

My eyes
I see everything
and yet nothing.

I've got my head on a swivel.
But I still see
nothing.

I'm up in a tree, high above the ground.
I see them all below me.
Laughing, yelling, walking together.
I observe and observe and observe
but I'm never a part of it.

Have you ever seen an owl join the party?
Have you ever even seen one on the ground?
I've got my head on a swivel
but I can only see behind me.

These wings could open, but I would only tumble awkwardly
to the ground, the humiliation sending me hurriedly
climbing back up, in a panic
to escape the mocking laughter and cold disapproval
of those who live down there.
It's happened so many times
before.

An empty breeze moves hollowly through these trees
and the trees, they silently shake.
The slightest dance of moving boughs, and waving leaves
but in the midst of this, there's just ... me.
I'm alone up here. And I haven't heard
any cries or calls that make sense to me
in a very long time.
There's no one else
here.

I think I'll just go back
in this tree hollow.

Workshop

Underground basement lab
Sick, twisted, cluttered workshop
Blood orange lighting
The master of this land works feverishly upon
the table.

A torn, ruined baby onesie. A tiny soul piece.
Along with maybe a memory.
It's withered and gray, sucked dry.
But this man pleads and growls and tries
to bring it back to life.

CPR, hooking up to devices, vigorous shaking
and howls for movement.
He needs to see it move, this thing
that he has kept for so long.
He wipes sweat from his brow as he struggles and
labors above this dead fragment.

We are witnessing a mad scientist here tonight, folks.
He wants to bring it back to life.
But for all the tools he has at his disposal
This laboratory still cannot reverse death.

He weeps to bring it back, to see that color and
light return.
But not to return it – no, to keep it.
There is no remorse here.
(or at least not enough to matter.)
This beast needs always to feed and if
this fragment is freed
he will howl with the agonized selfishness
of monsters who are too empty to care
about the proper owners of things.

This man is a black hole.
He exists to consume.

And when this soul piece goes back home
he will scream and weep
for himself.

Raining Gray

Gray day
Where nostalgia and repetition fall down upon the cement
I'm the only thing alive.
This universe is made up of me.
This rain and I
We're all there is.

Oh, I know
that if I were to look around with sharpened eye I
would pick out holes in this panorama.
Beneath weathered parts of this tapestry
red eyes out from under a tree
staring and smirking and coveting me.

There's monsters, everywhere. They're all around.
I feel like it's just them and me, all the other people I see
I think, they're just a mirage.
Sometimes.

But on this day where it's all gray
and perpetuity falls down upon the sidewalk
I feel safe, like I do when I'm hunkered down inside my mind.
I can tell myself, it's all just me
and, *for once,* I'm free to sit and think
without looking in fear around me.

Blasphemy

This outlandish, long-buried thought in me
has risen from a century-long dormancy
A thought that maybe, just maybe, I'm not helpless,
powerless, at the mercy of the world around me.

I know! I know – what ... blasphemy.
But the more I consider it, ponder it, turning
it over and over in my hands
the more I realize that this thought truly does
have the power to stand on its own.
It doesn't need my short-bitten, frightened
child's hands to hold it up
or some anxiously repeated reassurance
of its legitimacy to keep it steady.
This thought rises, undeniably and unstoppably,
and scorns the idea that it needs any validation
at all.

This was in me? I ask
but I already know the answer.
Underneath the denial, the terror, the long-dancing tremors
of self-hatred, shame, and chaos-inducing alters, the latter
holding onto parts of me that I felt too weak to acknowledge -
this thought was always here.

It's frightening to think
that maybe you do have control, after all.
What if I hurt people? the fat child babbles.
What if I turn into Dad? This monster inside of me –
Yes, this thought interrupts, dark eyes looking
thoughtfully.
There is a monster inside of me.
(There's a monster inside all of us.)
But whether I turn out like him
or like any of those others
is squarely up to me.
I have the control.

I will wield power over myself, over my circumstances,
and I will never hurt anyone on purpose.
I flat out, just – won't.
I have control over that too.

He had control over what he did.
He had excuses, and lies, to blame his behavior on
but it was never true.
He could have chosen to control the monster inside
and be a good man.
He could have done that
and chose to torment me
and others
instead.

I won't be like him.
I'm not him.
And I don't have to go through life an anxious victim
batting away anything resembling confidence
to achieve that.

Water from Stone

I have spent my whole life
trying to draw water from stone.
These sucking, empty entities, draining out your bones.
Hollowing them out, and then
sometimes
burrowing in and nesting in the spaces they've made there.

I am so sick and tired of feeling hollow in my bones.
The tighter I hold, the more I feel
alone.
There's nothing in these creatures, all they do is feed ...
and they will consume me to nothing while giving
nothing to me.

I have been changing. I know it in my bones.
This isn't me anymore, though
I still catch myself, looking down from that ledge
at all the things that want to hurt me,
if I just let them in.

I'm okay, I'm all right.
I think it's all behind me now.

I think I'm not afraid anymore.

This light, lightness, coming in and chasing the dark drudgery
out of my bones:
Maybe I'm allowed to be happy.

Comfort

Searching, always, for the strong reassuring arms
of one so much larger than me.
Looking for this, this comfort, perpetually, in every
social interaction.
I must always have these sad, large eyes cast upward,
must always have this lonely mouth cast downward.
Always hoping, in every Starbucks interaction, every customer
service call,
to find this reassuring presence
that has thus far always eluded me.

What kind of life is this? Always waiting for it to start.
Always standing in place, looking into the distance
for comfort from terrors that took place
centuries ago.
He was a control-obsessed monster. He terrorized me.
And when he was done he would just ... leave.
And, no, I of course don't have a time machine.
So this is just how it ... is.

There is no rescuer coming for me.
There is no external force soon to arrive
to reassure me, to tell me it's now safe to be alive.
The only larger ones that have come, and placed
their intent on me –
they were monsters too, and had no interest in comforting me.

I have to provide this comfort for myself.
I have to hold myself, and soothe myself when I cry.
It's such a sad, isolating thought, this thought
of being so alone ...
but this is how it's always been.
This isn't something new.
Waiting for eons, in the mouth of this dark cave, fantasizing
about companions that never arrive, and conversations that
never take place
All of my life I have been just as alone

as I am in this moment.

Giant

Searching for that giant face, blotting out the sun
- or rather, *is* the sun

Lost in fabric forests, underneath the world
Wake up, panicked, struggle to emerge
and start to breathe again.

Looking for a god, everywhere, in the faces of mere mortal men
Because faith is not an individual but a state of mind
and I'll never be two again.

The days of physical world and dreamscapes
interchangeable are far behind me now.
I am no longer a little traveler but merely a
spiritually bent earthbound.

Faith is not a person but a state of mind.
Or perhaps a necessary stage of development.
Looking for a god, in the faces of
what can be only mortal men.
What I am looking for is ever lost
because I'll never be two again.

Freeze and Strangulation

Sitting in the cold
But not the lonely outside cold, no.
That comforting cold in which you place things
that you love.
Things that you can't live without.

A dead body, plaid shirt and blue jeans.
Flat black beads looking out past.
Freezer burn on facial hair.
There's a couch that it's sitting on, head lolled back.
There's a table, and a chair
and blankets, and cards. Tea. A TV.
I love you so.

Keep it encased in ice. Some ugly things
have happened in here.
But you can't let them have it all.
The beauty outweighs it all
and this love, this unbreakable bond
outweighs everything that
has been done.

Do you understand what I am saying?
Do you understand that you have always been the universe
to me?
Do you understand?

If these caring gloved hands were to carry out an autopsy
they would undeniably find an empty hole where a soul
should be. A twisted, corrupted, sadistic mass
would have long since overtaken the cranial cavity, and
the heart would be a withered, stunted, pathetic thing
that scarce knew how to beat
when the body it belonged to was alive.
But these gloved hands, these understanding murderer's
hands, they would handle it all

and weep with empathy.

See? The examiner would say, to an audience or solely
to the room.
This is what happens when abused, broken things
are not able to overcome hideous beginnings.
And while this monstrosity has caused incalculable devastation
it still deserves love
and pity.
And I say that as the one who strangled the thing to death.

Am I frightening you?
I'm not trying to.
I'm trying only to say this to him – **I love you.**
But I **hate you**, too, because you molested and hurt and
dehumanized me.
I hate you with the unending well
belonging to those who love things that can't love them back.
I could be your murderer, I could be your M.E.
but I know that if I were to cut through these scrubs, through
my own chest cavity
I would find a needy black hole
where my soul should be.

- - - - - -

This all-enduring love
I keep it like a corpse, nice and cold
So it won't rot and wither.
Maybe someday I'll be able to turn off this refrigeration
and light, and leave this room and let
the whole thing decay.
Maybe the remembrance of this all-consuming love
will begin to fade.

But when that day comes I will no longer be
me.
Since the day I was born I have been intertwined
with this love and fear and hate and when it dies I will
no longer be
alive.

I'll be someone else then.
Even though you never deserved my love,
never did a thing to earn it
This loyalty to you, and compassion for your
suffering
I'm keeping it cold.
I'm keeping it cold for you.

... Or maybe more for me.
Maybe I'm just afraid
to die.

Because when you die in my heart I will die too.
But then I'll be ... someone new.
Maybe who
I was always meant to be.
Someone free, someone who does not weep
for what should have been, and sits eternally
in the cold.

- - - - - -

There's a letter, here, in a dusty desk
in an easily forgotten room.
It isn't as tragically tortured as the others,
so it gets ignored and removed
in favor of the louder messages that storm

and sob their way down these halls.
But this is what it reads.

I'm starting to wonder if this has more to do with identity.
Am I hurting so much all these years later because of what
he did to me?

Or just because I don't know who else to be?
Is this self-inflicted and
choking me?

Do I even love him still?

Buddy's Grove

Buddy
I love you.
I'm so grateful I got to meet you
and somewhere in Chippewa there's 16
trees named after you.

I still keep blankets and towels on all
your old sleeping spots.
Your urn and your photo book are still
on top of your cat tree.
The middle section still has those cards of
condolences, from the different vets' offices.
Leslie, she was the lady
that put you to sleep.
And then helped me get you out to the car
and hugged me in that introspective silence
of 1 am.
And then I brought
you
home.

But Buddy, I feel so awful –
the memories are starting to fade.
I know it's natural, but it's still so
cold and cruel.
It makes me feel like a monster.
I don't want to lose a single day we had.
I don't want to have to look at pictures
to remember your face.

I will never forget you, Buddy.
I'm so sorry I've started to lose some of
those days, but
My love for you will never fade.

I hope wherever you are
you're happy, and free.

I hope it's warm there, and that
you never have any reason to be afraid.
And I want you to know, Buddy,
that it's okay if you've started to forget
bits and pieces of me.
It's okay if my face has started to fade.
We're in different worlds now, and
with this kind of distance
I think it's inevitable.

But it *hurts*.

...
I wish you could come back!
I wish ...
I wish you could come back.
I wish I could have you back.
Sometimes I feel like you're so *close*, like if I could just
peer a little harder through this plane I could see you,
smiling and purring at me.
But it was time for you to start the next leg of
your journey, and ... it didn't include me.
I love you, Buddy.

I love you I love you I love you

Once

You have to hang on to the beautiful things.
You can't let them be consumed by the dark.
Let them ground you, and bring you home
when everything seems strange and lost.

I loved you once.
And it was beautiful, in spite
of what you did.
It doesn't matter if I love you now or not.
Because I had something beautiful once,
and I'll remember it forever.

I am so grateful
that I got to know what a love that deep felt like.
And for all your control and abuse
you'll never be able to take this from me.
You'll never be able to ruin the memory of how the world spun
      around you once.

I can discard this self-hatred, and obsessive
agony.
I can leave this behind, cast it all down except
how I once felt about you.
What I once suffered doesn't need to be my identity,
and rather than a death of myself
I feel like I've finally come home, at last.

It's not
THE END

www.ingramcontent.com/pod-product-compliance
Lightning Source LLC
Chambersburg PA
CBHW020429010526
44118CB00010B/487